WE ARE THE ANCIENT
EGYPTIANS

Meet the people behind the history

David Long

Illustrated by Allen Fatimaharan

WELBECK

Published in 2021 by Welbeck Children's Books

An imprint of Welbeck Children's Limited, part of Welbeck Publishing Group.
20 Mortimer Street, London W1T 3JW

Text © David Long 2021
Illustrations © Allen Fatimaharan 2021

Managing Art Editor: Matt Drew
Designer: Claire Clewley
Associate Publisher: Laura Knowles
Editor: Jenni Lazell

ISBN 978-1-78312-660-6

Printed in Heshan, China

10 9 8 7 6 5 4 3 2 1

Picture Credits:
pp56–57 Vector Art Design/Adobe Stock

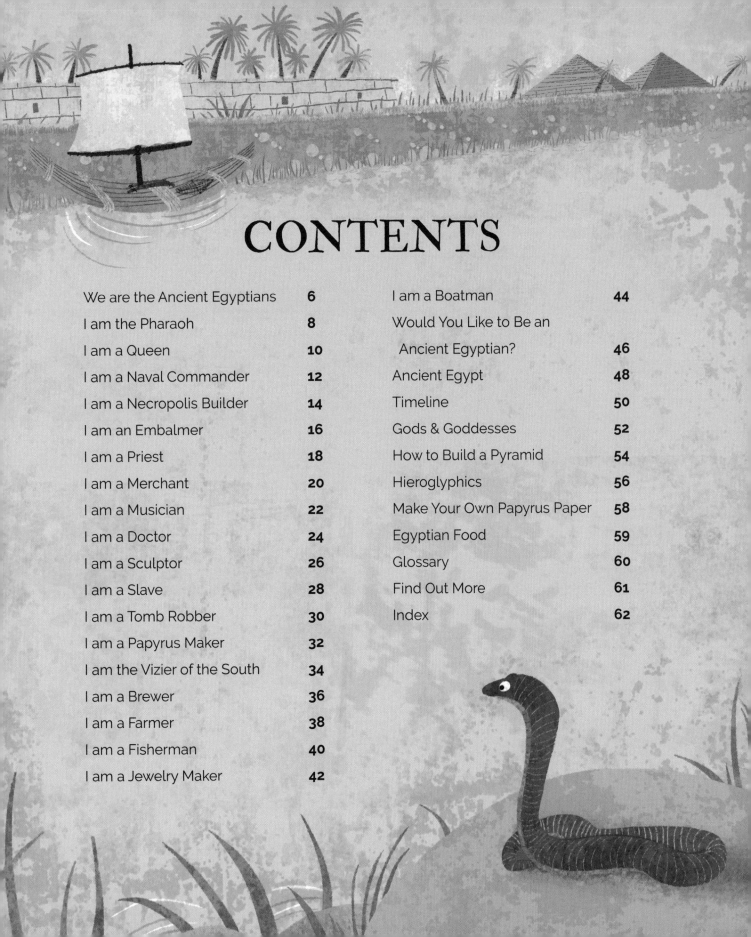

CONTENTS

WE ARE THE ANCIENT EGYPTIANS

 ← This means "Greetings" in hieroglyphics. You are about to set off on a tour of Ancient Egypt, but this isn't a tour of crumbling pyramids or shards of old pottery. No, instead you will meet people from Ancient Egypt. People who went to work or school, ate their dinner, and used the toilet. In lots of ways, the lives of Ancient Egyptians were just the same as yours, but in other ways, they were very different. We hope you enjoy getting to know us!

WHO WERE THE ANCIENT EGYPTIANS?

The people we call the Ancient Egyptians lived along the banks of the Nile in northern Africa. The Nile is longest river in the world and the first farmers settled in this region more than 7,000 years ago. Fertile land along the river and good trade with neighboring countries led to a rich and powerful civilization. This was ruled by pharaohs and lasted for around 3,000 years.

The Egyptians that we know the most about were pharaohs and other rich and important people. However, we also know a lot about how ordinary Egyptian families lived. They enjoyed music and dancing, they liked colorful makeup and wigs (even the men!) and many of them wore perfume and elaborate jewelry. Ordinary Egyptians worshipped hundreds of different gods, and Egyptian artists produced many fine stone statues and other beautiful objects.

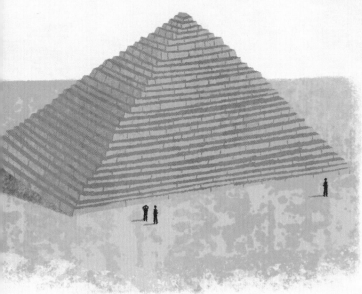

WHAT WERE THE ANCIENT EGYPTIANS FAMOUS FOR?

The Ancient Egyptians built the largest buildings the world had ever seen. The most famous are the pyramids, which were built as royal tombs and are still standing today. They also created a sophisticated way of writing (using simple pictures called hieroglyphics) and were very good at mathematics. Most writing was done on a type of paper called papyrus, made from the reeds growing along the Nile. This was much lighter and easier to use than the clay tablets that people had used before.

WHAT DO WE OWE TO THE ANCIENT EGYPTIANS?

The Ancient Egyptians were great at inventing things. These were the first people to make plows that could be pulled by animals and to use special curved blades for harvesting crops. They invented colored inks, a solar calendar to measure the seasons using the Sun, and at least two different types of clock. One was a sort of sundial and the other indicated the time by measuring the rate at which water emptied through a tiny hole in a special bowl. The first ever toothpaste was Egyptian, too. It was made by mixing salt, mint, dried flowers, and grains of pepper, but no one makes it this way today.

Ancient Egyptian sundial

I AM THE PHARAOH

I am Thutmose III and I rule over all of Egypt. My stepmother Hatshepsut was on the throne before me, although female pharaohs have always been very unusual.

Hatshepsut ruled the country instead of me because I was only a baby when my father died. She was clever and she trained me carefully for my official roles. As I grew older she made me head of the army.

I enjoyed military life. I was good at horse riding and my skill as an archer helped to win many battles against Egypt's enemies. The army under my command captured 350 cities and conquered more countries in Africa and the Middle East than any other pharaoh. This made the kingdom larger and richer than it had ever been before.

I used to hunt elephants as a way of relaxing but now I am too old to do this. I have reigned for 54 years, which is almost a record for a pharaoh.

It is normal for Egyptian rulers to have several wives at the same time, so I have four who are Egyptian and another three who came from Asia. Between us, we have many children and I had always hoped that the first boy would be pharaoh after me. Unfortunately, Amenemhat died when he was a young man so his brother Amenhotep will rule Egypt when I am dead.

My people still call me "the Warrior" because I have never lost a battle, but I am just as proud of my other achievements. I have paid for more than fifty temples and shrines to be built, including the enormous Festival Hall at Karnak. This is one of Egypt's most important religious centers and I chose it as a place to worship more than sixty of my ancestors.

I AM A QUEEN

The Pharaoh has many wives, but I am the most important one. That is why the people call me "The Great Royal Wife," although my actual name is Satiah.

Satiah means "Daughter of the Moon God," but my real mother was a nurse who looked after the young princes in the royal palace. My father was a more important person: he was a high-ranking adviser to my husband and before this he served under no fewer than five previous pharaohs. Both my parents are dead now.

Women play an important part in Egyptian society. We are not just wives and mothers and many women own and run successful businesses. Others work as weavers or priestesses, and a few hold important government posts although this is quite unusual. One of the ways I help the Pharaoh is by interpreting or explaining his

dreams. We Egyptians believe dreams give us a chance to meet gods and to talk to our ancestors. Men and women often go to special buildings to sleep because they believe they will have more dreams inside one of these than if they stay at home. One of the buildings is attached to the Temple of Hathor. It is very popular and has dark, underground chambers where dreamers can stay for the night.

Dreams can help us see what is going to happen in the future but the messages we receive this way can often be confusing. Women like me are skilled at explaining the things that people remember when they wake up after a dream. Sometimes the Pharaoh's dreams bring him bad news, but at other times they let him know that he will win another important battle or show him a good place to build a new temple to the gods.

I AM A NAVAL COMMANDER

Egypt's military forces fight many battles on land and at sea, and I serve the Pharaoh by commanding a fleet of ships in his great navy.

My name is Ptahhotep and the men I command go to sea in vessels called *kebentiu*. These have a sail as well as thirty strong oarsmen, which makes them much faster than the ships of our enemies. The two largest oars are at the back and are used to steer the ship during a battle. Once it is in the right position, archers onboard can fire hundreds of arrows with deadly accuracy.

Years ago, when I first joined the navy, all of our ships were quite small. Most battles took place on land and the ships were just used to transport soldiers to wherever our enemies were. Now, though, navy vessels are built for fighting at sea. They are made of cedarwood which means they are larger and faster than before. Wood from cedar trees is hard and strong but it is also more expensive because the finest ships require the best wood from the biggest trees. Most of this has to come from other countries because very few trees grow in a hot, desert country like Egypt.

All soldiers and sailors know that in battle it is important to surprise the enemy. Once I ordered my men to carry an entire ship across dry land from one river to another. It was hard work in the heat and it took more than two days, but my cunning plan worked perfectly. While our enemies looked for us in the desert, we were able to sneak up and surprise them by attacking from behind. It was a proud moment for the navy and for me, Ptahhotep. An important battle was won thanks to my idea and the bravery of my men.

I AM A NECROPOLIS BUILDER

My name is User and I am in charge of building grand tombs for members of Egypt's royal family and the very rich.

For hundreds of years, our ancestors built pyramids to contain the bodies of dead pharaohs and their families. These are the tallest buildings in the world, but thousands of men were needed to build each one and the work took many years to complete. Now we prefer different types of tomb which are mostly hidden underground or cut deep into the solid rock of high cliffs. The finest ones are in an area of the desert called the Valley of the Kings.

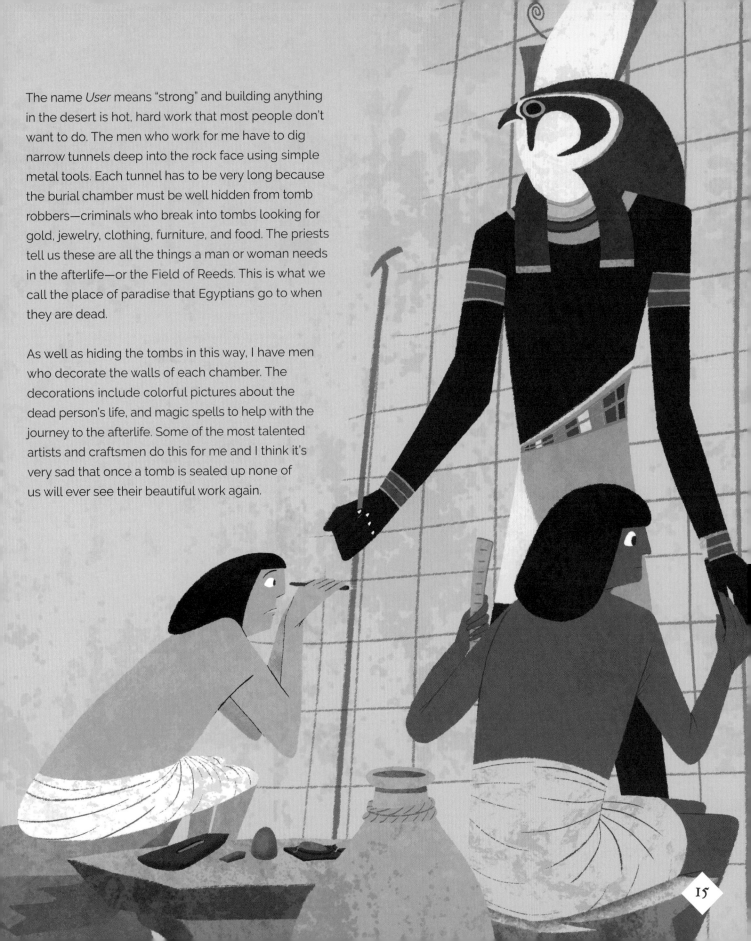

The name *User* means "strong" and building anything in the desert is hot, hard work that most people don't want to do. The men who work for me have to dig narrow tunnels deep into the rock face using simple metal tools. Each tunnel has to be very long because the burial chamber must be well hidden from tomb robbers—criminals who break into tombs looking for gold, jewelry, clothing, furniture, and food. The priests tell us these are all the things a man or woman needs in the afterlife—or the Field of Reeds. This is what we call the place of paradise that Egyptians go to when they are dead.

As well as hiding the tombs in this way, I have men who decorate the walls of each chamber. The decorations include colorful pictures about the dead person's life, and magic spells to help with the journey to the afterlife. Some of the most talented artists and craftsmen do this for me and I think it's very sad that once a tomb is sealed up none of us will ever see their beautiful work again.

I AM AN EMBALMER

My name is Nebamun and when a rich man or woman dies I prepare the body for burial.

Egyptians believe that when people die and go to the Field of Reeds they still need their body. Because of this we take great care to preserve each body before it is buried. We call this mummification. Preparing a mummy is a complicated process but an important one. People admire me for the quality of my work.

Mostly I work in a special tent called an *ibu*. My assistants first wash the body using water from the Nile and wine made from palm trees. A small cut is then made in one side of the body so the lungs and other internal organs can be taken out. These are then covered in something called natron, which is a kind of salt found in the desert. It dries out the organs and stops them from going moldy. I also remove the brain by using a long metal hook to pull it out through the dead person's nose.

More natron is stuffed into the body which is then left to dry for 40 days. It is then washed again and the skin is rubbed with sweet-smelling oil. The organs are wrapped in a type of cloth called linen. Our ancestors used to put them in containers called canopic jars which are decorated with the animal heads of our gods. These days they are put back into the body so the person will have everything he or she needs in the Field of Reeds.

The body is then carefully wrapped using more linen cut into long strips. Every part of the mummy is wrapped, including each individual finger and toe, so it takes a long time. I paint the strips with a sticky juice from pine trees. This is called resin and it makes the strips hard.

I also hide magic charms called amulets between the strips to bring good luck. After this the body is put into a beautifully painted wooden sarcophagus or coffin, and then inside an even larger one carved from stone. Often an artist will paint a face on the wooden one to show what the person used to look like. Our work is very skilled.

I AM A PRIEST

My name is Herhut and one of my jobs is to say prayers over the bodies of the dead while they are being mummified and prepared for burial.

Prayers and spells are an important part of mummification and we say them out loud to ensure that the dead person reaches the afterlife safely. Priests like me take great care to speak clearly and to make sure that exactly the right words are used. None of the prayers and spells would work if I said them in the wrong way.

In Egypt, priests are called Servants of the Gods because Egyptians worship many different gods. Because of this, there are different kinds of priests. Nearly all of us are men although women can also be priests and there are a few at the temple where I live.

High priests are some of the most important people in the country and they are chosen by the pharaoh himself. Other, less important priests take care of the temples. These priests help with the preparations for religious festivals that take place throughout the year. Rich families pay some of them to say prayers for the family's dead relatives.

At my temple we also have a special priest called an hour-priest. He studies the stars at night and can tell which days of the year will be lucky and which ones will be unlucky. We also have lector priests who write religious documents and speak at festivals. The lector priests have their own secret places in the temple that women priests are not allowed to enter.

Every day there are different religious rituals to perform at the temple, so priests and priestesses are always busy. Often we are accompanied by singers and musicians, and many different gods are worshipped in this way. Egyptians worship so many different gods that no one knows the actual number. I think it is probably about 2,000, but it could be a lot more.

I AM A MERCHANT

My name is Senna and I am a successful merchant. Egypt is a great trading nation and has been for hundreds of years. We have grown rich by selling goods to other countries, and by bringing back what they have to sell.

This is all done by barter, which means exchanging one thing for another instead of buying it with money. For example, I once exchanged some small pieces of gold jewelry for enough wood to build a ship. Another time I swapped a hundred sacks of grain (for making bread) for large clay pots full of wine. When Egypt has too much of something, a good merchant can always find someone, somewhere else who wants it. They will offer him something valuable or useful in return.

Being a merchant means I travel a lot, which I enjoy, except that I miss my wife Ahit and our children. I travel with other merchants so we can protect ourselves from robbers and bandits. We ride our camels to the busy ports on the Red Sea where traders from other countries come to unload their ships.

The journey can take many days but it is worth it if
I return with goods that I can sell in the market. My
favorites are small items that I can hide in my clothes.
Rare spices, pieces of elephant ivory, and beautiful,
precious stones are the best—especially blue lapis lazuli
and bright green malachite. If I buy anything larger I have
to hire carts and more camels from my friend, Takhaet.
He laughs when I have to do this but it means I make
less profit and the journey home takes even longer.

Whatever I bring back, I sell at the market near to where I
live in the town of Waset. Ordinary Egyptians shop at the
market for everything from food to clothing and cooking
pots. It is a noisy place and very busy but I enjoy being
there. I see my friends and the customers all know me.

I AM A MUSICIAN

My name is Tat-Akat and I am always working because music and dancing are very popular in Egypt.

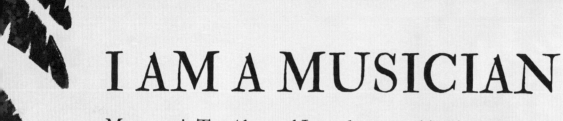

You will always hear music at official celebrations. Musicians will also often play in the street for passers-by who give food or some other little gift if they enjoy what we play for them. Professional musicians like me perform in the temples as well as during military parades and sometimes even at the Pharaoh's court. My friends and I have also played at many great banquets for rich and important people. The guests at these banquets never dance but they like us to bring along dancers and acrobats so they can sit back and watch.

I learned to play from my mother who taught me nearly a hundred different tunes. Nothing was written down, but she played while I watched and then I copied her until I got it right. I began as a child with drums and rattles while she plucked the strings of a spike-lute made from goatskin and a polished turtle shell. She let me try the lute when I was older but it took years for my playing to be as beautiful as hers. Now it is my favorite instrument, although I still enjoy playing the drums.

I often perform with my friend Rimes who has a silver trumpet that he is very proud of. He has promised to teach me how to play it one day but only if I show him how to play my mother's lute. Rimes works hard like me, and he is very talented, but I think his hands are too big for him to become a really good lute player. When I tell him this he laughs and says I have a face like a baboon.

I AM A DOCTOR

My name is Naa. I heal the sick and treat their injuries.

I am unusual because most doctors in Egypt are men. No one knows why this is, and I do know a few people who still think men make the best doctors. Fortunately, not everyone agrees with this, so I always have a long line of patients waiting to see me.

Examining the body during mummification has shown us some of the ways the body works. Doctors know the heart pumps blood through veins around the body, and we understand how to tightly bandage broken bones to help them mend properly. The brain is still a mystery though, and many of us think it has no real use at all.

Even with the knowledge we have, we still use magic as well as mixtures or potions to treat people who are injured or sick. Sometimes I give patients herbs and spices that I have ground up with honey, beer, or wine. Other times I say prayers out loud and use secret spells.

Some of the remedies are my own invention but others are ones I have copied out from ancient papyrus scrolls. These were written by our ancestors, other doctors like me, and they are kept in a special part of the temple called the *Per-Ankh*. This means the "House of Life" and the scrolls there contain details about the medicines and treatments that our ancestors found most helpful for a quick recovery.

I have also used rituals involving gods and goddesses. If someone is stung by a poisonous scorpion, for example, I call up to the goddess Serket. Another, called Tawreret, helps me when a mother or a new baby gets sick. I often ask Heka to help me. She is the goddess of magic and medicine.

I AM A SCULPTOR

When I carve my name in stone it says "Silsi the Sculptor" because that is who I am.

My father was a sculptor, too, and so was his father before him. That is how things work in Egypt. Parents teach their children, and then the children grow up and teach their own children, and so on. Skills, crafts, and even jobs pass down through families in this way and often this has happened for many, many generations.

Two of my ancestors carved statues and stone coffins for important royal princes and for more than two years I have been working on a giant coffin for the Pharaoh himself. Of course he is not dead yet, and I pray that all the gods and goddesses will keep him safe for many years. But carving a sarcophagus takes a long time so it is important to start early.

I think it is my best carving so far. The stone is the finest we could find anywhere in the kingdom. It is a rich red-brown and as hard as a jewel. This makes my work more difficult

than usual but the sarcophagus will last well as a result. It will last longer than anything carved from a cheaper, softer stone, and much, much longer than a man's lifespan.

My children are still young and wanted me to carve chickens into the stone because they know the Pharaoh has the only hens in the whole of Egypt. This would not be allowed though, so I have decorated it with the Pharaoh's favorite gods, which is the custom. I will also carve magical Eyes of Horus on the side of the sarcophagus because Egyptians believe the mummy needs these to look out at the world.

Yesterday I was told that the Pharaoh has heard of my work and is pleased with its high quality. When I am finished, he says, he wants me to make two large stone obelisks for his new temple at Heliopolis. There is always work in Egypt for a good sculptor so I am never idle.

I AM A SLAVE

I am Layla the slave and I have been owned by my mistress for as long as I can remember.

I live in her house which is very large and has two floors. It has more than twenty rooms and the outside is painted white every year by one of the older slaves. He once told me this helps to keep the house cool by reflecting the sun's heat. Another slave said this too, but the kitchen where I work is always hot because the oven is heated by a fire.

I work every day and hardly ever go outside unless it is to carry things back from the market for my mistress. Mostly I am in the kitchen making fresh bread and cakes. All Egyptians eat a lot of bread. My mistress and her family have it with every meal so there is a lot of baking to do.

My first job is to make flour, usually by grinding emmer wheat between two large stones. Sometimes I use barley instead, another crop which grows well in Egypt. Unfortunately, grains of sand from the desert often blow into the flour making it gritty. This is bad for our teeth and my mistress gets angry, although she knows it is not my fault.

After I've ground the flour, I mix it with water in a large bowl to produce dough. This takes a long time to do properly so when my hands get tired I put the bowl on the floor and use my feet.

Normal loaves are round and flat but sometimes my mistress wants the dough formed into different shapes before it is baked. She likes tall, cone-shaped loaves but my favorites are the ones I mold to look like fish or crocodiles. When the family want different flavors, I mix the dough with coriander seeds, herbs, or honey before cooking it. Sweet fruits, such as figs and dates also make delicious bread but only a rich family like this one can afford to eat these.

I AM A TOMB ROBBER

I don't tell anyone my real name because robbing graves is a serious crime in Egypt and I don't want to get caught.

My gang and I make a good living by stealing but the risks are very high. Two men we knew were caught robbing a grave last winter. Both were whipped a hundred times with a cane outside the temple and then held underwater until they were dead. Another time I watched a thief having his head cut off on the orders of the Pharaoh.

I didn't used to do this. I was an honest man to begin with. One of my jobs was digging out burial chambers and I saw how much treasure gets buried with the dead. Once I saw a little mirror that was solid gold and another tomb had more things in it than my family has ever owned. Expensive luxuries were piled up to the ceiling so you can hardly blame me for wanting some of them for myself.

Robbing a tomb is never easy though. The priests have the entrance blocked up with piles of heavy stones when they seal a tomb shut. We have to carry these out by hand which is hard work and dangerous. If we get trapped or injured by falling rocks, there's no one around to get us out. Also, my gang has to work at night when there are wild animals about. We hear jackals howling in the desert and I worry all the time about treading on a venomous snake.

Sometimes all this work is for nothing. Last year we spent more than twenty-five days clearing rocks only to find the burial chamber was completely empty. Another gang must have gotten there first and taken everything, or maybe the dead man's family had secretly moved the treasures to another secret tomb to stop it being discovered by thieves like me.

I AM A PAPYRUS MAKER

My name is Bak and I make papyrus for people to write on. Most Egyptians can't read or write so they pay scribes to do this for them. The scribes come to me when they need to write a letter or a document.

My father taught me how to make it when I was a boy and his old workshop now belongs to me. He used to harvest bright green reeds from the muddy banks of the great Nile river. Most days there are reedsellers in the marketplace, but I prefer to harvest my own and bring them back to the workshop.

The reeds are tall and tough, so the first thing I do is peel away the outer layer. The inside is a pale, creamier color and I carefully cut this into long, thin strips with my metal knife. The best strips come from the very center of the plant. I put these into a large dish of water and leave them for several days.

32

The strips are bendy and almost transparent when I take them out of the water. This is how I want them. While they are still wet, I bash them again and again with a flat stone. Strips that are as thin and as flat as possible make the best papyrus.

Before the strips dry out, I weave them together into neat squares. The strips must be kept close together with no gaps or holes between them. Their natural stickiness helps the square stay in one piece while I place it between layers of linen cloth and two wooden boards. I weigh the top board down with more heavy stones to flatten the square, and then leave everything in place for another week to dry out properly. After this, I polish the square piece of papyrus by rubbing it hard with the back of an old, smooth seashell. The papyrus is then ready for a scribe to write on.

33

I AM THE VIZIER OF THE SOUTH

I am Rekhmire and for many years I have been the Pharaoh's chief minister.

Egypt was already too large to be governed by one man when Thutmose III began his reign. Since then, he and his armies have made it even larger by conquering many big cities that belonged to our neighbors. Now two senior officials are needed to run the country for the Pharaoh, and we are known as viziers.

I am in charge of the south of the country, and my friend Neferweben is responsible for the north. This means we are very important men and no one in the whole of Egypt has more power than us except the Pharaoh himself. Neferweben and I speak to the Pharaoh several times a week and he trusts us to run the country in the way he wants it to be run. We each have hundreds of officials to help us do this because organizing the lives of more than a million people is a very complicated task.

My grandfather and my uncle were viziers before me and I learned a lot from them both. They ran the courts where criminals were tried, and decided on the punishments of those who were found guilty. Now I do this too. I also make sure that people pay their taxes every year, and when the Pharaoh spends huge amounts of gold on temples and other great buildings, it is my job to see that none of it is wasted or gets stolen.

Laws are important in a civilized country like Egypt and I am a strict man who likes to see that the laws are obeyed. However, I try to be fair. Ordinary people can come to me with their problems, for example, when one farmer says another has moved on to his land without permission. I listen to both sides of the argument and decide who is right and who is wrong.

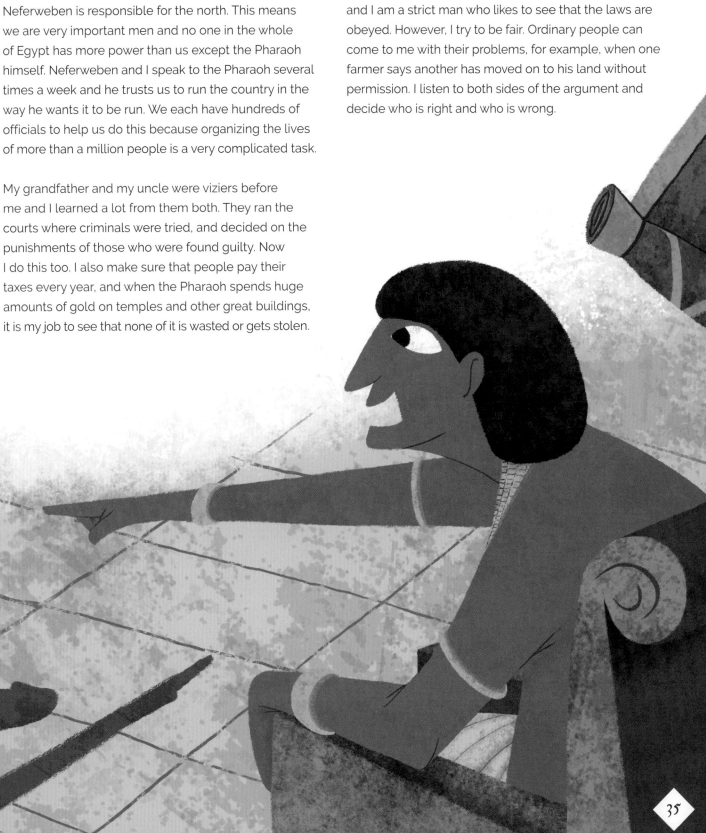

I AM A BREWER

I make beer to sell in jugs at the market, and my name is Shadya.

Egyptians all drink beer, even small children. Everyone knows that animals live in the river (and that people wash in it) so drinking the water can make them sick. Beer is much safer so all of us drink it several times a day. Rich people drink it too, although at banquets and feasts they often have wine, which is red like blood. Their wine is made from grapes or figs and is expensive.

The beer I make is much cheaper, so people buy a lot of it. It is sweet and thicker than wine, a bit like runny porridge. I make it using emmer wheat or barley grains and tell my customers that it is nutritious as well as delicious. Workers' wages often include three jugs of beer a day, and some of them say mine gives them the energy they need to keep going until they can stop for food.

Most brewers are women like me and we all have our favorite recipes. We keep these secret, although everyone starts the same way by mixing the wheat or barley grains in warm water and adding some mashed up pieces of old bread. The bread contains something called yeast that makes the water mixture fizz and ferment. This turns it into beer, although no one really understands how.

I mix mine in large clay pots at home. After a few days, I add different flavors such as pistachio nuts, rose petals, cilantro, or a sweet-smelling spice like cumin. Most customers drink it through a straw. This stops them from swallowing the pieces of bread and grain which sink to the bottom of the pot.

I AM A FARMER

My name is Nykara and for most of the year I am busy growing crops on the banks of the river Nile.

The great river floods the fields every year. When this happens I travel into a nearby town where I find work as a builder or workman. I only come back when the fields begin to dry out. The floods leave behind a new layer of rich, fertile soil on the land. It looks almost black but is good for growing wheat to make bread as well as the onions, leeks, and beans that my family likes to eat.

Most years the harvest is good unless the sun makes the soil too dry before the next flood. The crops die if that happens and we don't have enough food.

Farmers like me divide the year into three different seasons. The first is called *akhet,* which is when the fields flood. The second is *peret* and this is when I plow the fields and plant the seeds for new crops. The third is *shemu,* harvest-time, when the crops ripen and I cut them down. I then store them and wait for the next flood to come.

Most of the time I enjoy being a farmer. It is better than doing building work although it is exhausting because I have only simple tools made of wood or stone. I have bought a couple of oxen this year to pull my old plow, but otherwise there is no one to help except my children. The only other animals are a goat, two fat pigs, and some noisy geese. We will eat these on special occasions.

I also helped my neighbor make a *shaduf* for watering our fields when the weather is at its hottest. Long ditches bring water from the river into the fields and the shaduf is the best way to lift the water up and into clay pots. The water can then be used to stop the crops from drying out before they are ripe and ready to be harvested.

I AM A FISHERMAN

I am Anpet. I used to fish in the river Nile with my father and now I do it with my son Ti. We sell most of what we catch at the market but keep some of it for ourselves.

We are lucky that the Nile is such a big river and that it has so many different fish living in it, as we Egyptians eat a lot of fish. Fishermen have special names for all of them, including cat fish, tiger fish, elephant fish, moon fish, and puffer fish. We catch these all the time as well as perch, tilapia, mullet, carp, and eels, which are just as good to eat. Unfortunately, there are also crocodiles in the river, which are bigger than I am. They will attack us if we are not careful.

When Ti was very little he used to spend most days chasing frogs and blue dragonflies but now he is a good boy and works hard with me. On the bank each morning we pray to the fish-goddess Hatmehit and then decide which method is best to catch which sort of fish.

I throw a sharp spear into the water if we spot really big fish, but these are very fast-moving and I usually miss. Our net is much better for smaller fish or we use long lines with weights made of clay. The lines are fixed to tiny metal hooks made of bronze. We hide the hooks inside small balls of bread which I chew first to make them sticky. Egyptian hooks have a sharp tip called a barb and when a fish swallows the bread we can pull it out of the water. I kill each fish by hitting it on the head. Ti doesn't like this but he is getting used to it now.

Most of the fish we sell gets boiled or roasted over a fire but we dry some of it in the Sun or cover it with salt. This stops it from going bad quickly so it can be stored for eating later.

I AM A JEWELRY MAKER

My name is Aahhotep and I have spent more than twenty years making and selling jewelry.

Nearly everyone in Egypt likes to wear jewelry and colorful makeup. This includes men as well as women and many small children. Most ordinary Egyptians cannot afford gold or silver like Pharaoh and his family wear so I make a lot of my jewelry using copper and colored beads. I polish these until they shine like real gemstones. The copper comes from mines in the Nubian desert. It is of very high quality and I use it to make bracelets, earrings, anklets, armbands, and rings. The largest things I make are wide collars and necklaces. Sometimes I am asked to decorate them with beads made of colored glass

but these can be expensive because Egyptians have only recently started making glass. It is very fashionable and I am hoping it will get cheaper as more people learn how to make it by melting sand in a fire.

Animal shapes are another popular decoration, especially jackals, tigers, and winged birds. I also make a lot of scarabs, which are small stones carved to look like beetles. Although they seem very simple they take a long time to finish because the stone is so hard. My favorite stones have always been red carnelian and black obsidian but these are too expensive for most of my customers.

The scarabs I carve are usually oval and people keep them as good luck charms. However, if somebody asks me for one which is heart-shaped instead, I know it is going to be buried with a member of his family. This doesn't happen very often but when it does I take extra care while I am working to make the finest scarab possible.

I AM A BOATMAN

I am Nortat the boatman and I work on the Nile.

I used to have an old-fashioned boat called a skiff that I made by tying many bundles of reeds together with ropes made from more reed. I cut the reeds down myself so it was very cheap to build. The anchor was just an old piece of stone which I found lying around and tied up with rope.

My old skiff still floated after many years. It was easy to repair but it was small and couldn't carry much. Now I have a larger boat made of wood and I use it to carry passengers on the river as well as cargo. Boats like mine are very important in Egypt because the river provides the easiest way to travel around. Today I am transporting several heavy clay jars full of olive oil. I also have some baskets made of reed and a naughty pig that keeps trying to eat the baskets.

The river does most of the work for me when I am traveling northward because it flows in that direction towards the great, green sea we call Uat-Ur. When the time comes to travel back home again, I use a sail to catch the wind, which usually blows in the right direction. Moving the heavy wooden oar at the back steers the boat left or right. This is important because the river is always busy and I don't want to hit any of the boats coming the other way.

Last year I saw Pharaoh Thutmose on his boat. Of course it is much larger than mine, and covered in gold and colorful decorations. The Great Ruler was sitting beneath a shade so I couldn't see him properly, but I watched a crew of ten strong slaves pulling on the oars. The boat was moving along at a tremendous speed and before long it had disappeared. That was the only time I ever saw the Pharaoh.

WOULD YOU LIKE TO BE AN ANCIENT EGYPTIAN?

You've met a powerful pharaoh and a hardworking slave girl, a boatman who travels the Nile, and a tomb robber, risking his life to steal treasure. Now you've got to know a few of them, would *you* like to try your luck at living life as an Ancient Egyptian?

What you might have noticed from this book is that there were lots of differences between the lives of different Ancient Egyptians. Some were powerful and able to lead easier lives, whereas others had to work hard under the hot sun to put food on the table for their family. But they all

tried to lead a good life and live it to the fullest, so they could enter the afterlife when they died.

Living close to the Nile meant Ancient Egyptians had great access to fertile soil and trade along the river. It was a prosperous civilization. But the life you led was determined strictly by your social class—there wasn't a lot of social mobility. If you were born into a peasant family and lived in a mud brick house, it's unlikely you could become anything else.

So if you could go back in time and try being an Ancient Egyptian for yourself, you'd need to weigh the advantages and disadvantages of being a powerful vizier or a talented artist. But while you might be entertained by musicians, enjoy a trip up the Nile, or gaze at beautiful sculptures, you would be a few thousand years too early to order take-out, play games on your phone, and text your friends!

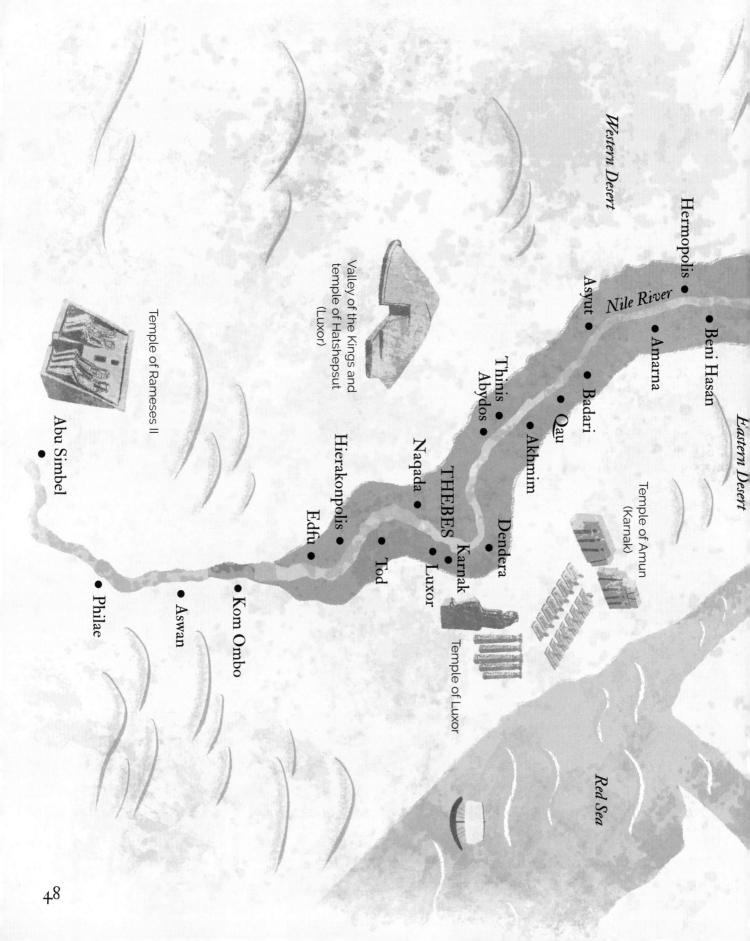

Western Desert

Eastern Desert

Hermopolis

Nile River

Asyut

Amarna

Beni Hasan

Thinis
Abydos

Badari

Qau

Akhmim

Valley of the Kings and
temple of Hatshepsut
(Luxor)

Naqada

THEBES

Temple of Amun
(Karnak)

Temple of Rameses II

Hierakonpolis

Karnak

Dendera

Luxor

Temple of Luxor

Abu Simbel

Edfu

Tod

Kom Ombo

Aswan

Philae

Red Sea

ANCIENT EGYPT

Surrounded by deserts, the great civilization of Ancient Egypt was built on fertile land along the river Nile, and lasted for over three thousand years.

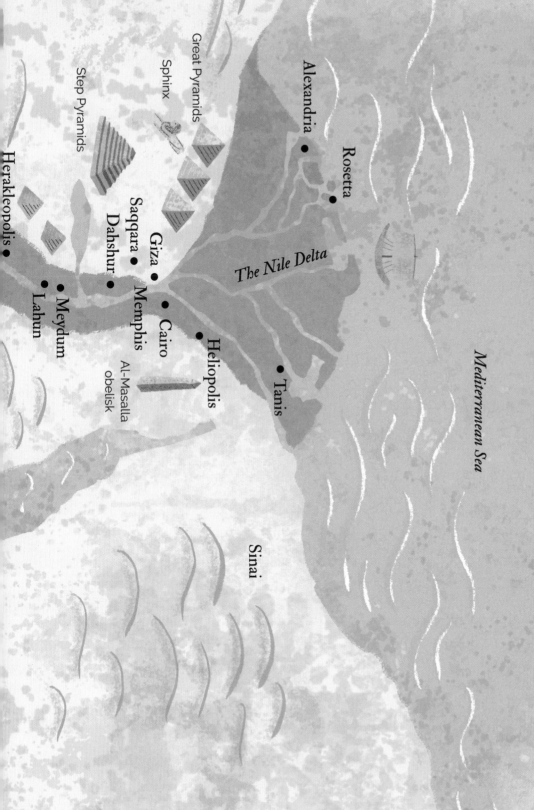

Mediterranean Sea

Alexandria

Rosetta

The Nile Delta

Tanis

Sinai

Heliopolis

Al-Masalla obelisk

Cairo

Memphis

Giza

Saqqara

Dahshur

Meydum

Lahun

Great Pyramids

Sphinx

Step Pyramids

Herakleopolis

TIMELINE

Read about the key points in Ancient Egyptian history, from the settling of its people along the Nile to finally being conquered by the Roman Empire.

6000 BCE

People began to settle in the Nile Valley. Most were farmers, hunters, and fishermen but some began to use clay from the banks of the river to make pots.

5000 BCE

Farming was becoming more sophisticated. As well as raising sheep and cattle, Egyptians began growing crops such as wheat and barley.

4500 BCE

The Nile was the most important transport route in Egypt. Reed boats were fitted with sails for the first time. This enabled boatmen to travel faster and more easily than before.

1479 BCE

Thutmose III began his long reign as pharaoh. He was a brilliant and courageous military commander and his conquests made the kingdom of Egypt larger than it had ever been before.

1550 BCE

The first royal tombs were built in the Valley of the Kings. These were hidden from view in an attempt to avoid their treasures being stolen by tomb robbers.

2500 BCE

Egyptians began making papyrus for the first time. Meanwhile early Britons completed the ceremonial stone circle known as Stonehenge and the Chinese began producing cloth using silkworms.

1325 BCE

Tutankhamun was buried in the Valley of the Kings. He hadn't ruled for long but the gold and other treasures discovered in his tomb have made him one of the most famous pharaohs of them all.

1279 BCE

The reign of Ramesses II began. He ruled Egypt for 67 years, longer than any other pharaoh, and is believed to have had more than 100 children.

750 BCE

The city of Rome was founded in what is now Italy. What had once been a small farming village went on to become the center of the vast Roman Empire.

4000 BCE

The Egyptians began to make jewelry using gold, silver, and copper. Farming in Britain began around the same time, probably started by settlers who arrived by boat from elsewhere in Europe.

3500 BCE

Wall paintings began to include hieroglyphics, the symbols used for Egyptian writing. A thousand miles away in Mesopotamia (modern day Iraq) people began using some of the first wheeled vehicles.

3100 BCE

The regions of Upper Egypt and Lower Egypt were joined to create a single country ruled by the first pharaoh, a warrior called Narmer.

2600 BCE

Egyptians began building vast stone pyramids as royal tombs. They also made the Great Sphinx of Giza, the world's largest sculpture, depicting a creature with the body of a lion and the head of a human.

2800 BCE

Lamps burning olive oil provided a source of light after sunset. People began growing grapes on vines and using them to make wine.

3000 BCE

The first villages and towns were constructed, with buildings made of bricks formed from mud from the river. The mud was mixed with straw to make it stronger and then baked hard in the sun.

322 BCE

Egypt was conquered by Alexander the Great, a brilliant Greek military commander with a large and powerful army.

196 BCE

Lettering in three different languages was carved on to a black monument known today as the Rosetta Stone. Its discovery in the 18th century enabled experts to finally decode Egyptian hieroglyphics.

51 BCE

Egypt was ruled by Cleopatra, the last pharaoh and one of just six or seven women to sit on the throne. After her death in 30 BCE, Egypt became a part of the Roman Empire.

GODS & GODDESSES

Ancient Egyptians worshipped thousands of gods, who often took the form of animals. People prayed to them for guidance and protection, and kept them happy with rituals and offerings.

RA

God of the Sun and kings. Ra was one of the most important Egyptian gods who ruled over the sky, the Earth and the underworld. Egyptian kings believed themselves descended from Ra.

Appearance: Head of a falcon, body of a man

NUT

Nut was one of the oldest Egyptian deities whose body formed the sky and stars. She swallowed the Sun each evening and gave birth to it every morning.

Appearance: Woman covered in stars

HATHOR

Goddess of women, fertility, and love. Hathor was also associated with music and dance, and welcomed the dead into the next life.

Appearance: Woman, cow, or cow-headed woman

ANUBIS

Anubis was the god of the dead and mummification, who guarded tombs and guided souls to the afterlife. Anubis helped decide if a soul would enter the afterlife or be devoured.

Appearance: Head of a jackal, body of a man

MA'AT

Goddess of truth, justice, and cosmic order. Ma'at weighed the hearts of the dead against one of her feathers. Only hearts the same weight or lighter than the feather would go to the afterlife.

Appearance: Woman with wings on each arm

PTAH

Ptah thought himself into being and supposedly built the Universe, too. He was the patron of sculptors, builders, painters, and other crafts.

Appearance: Sometimes shown as a dwarf, or as a mummy with green skin

HORUS

Horus was a sky god, whose right eye was meant to be the Sun and his left eye the Moon. He was a patron of pharoahs. The "Eye of Horus" is an ancient symbol of protection meant to ward off evil.

Appearance: Head of a falcon, body of a man

THOTH

God of wisdom, knowledge, and the Moon, Thoth was the inventor of hieroglyphics and was both the scribe and advisor of the gods.

Appearance: Head of an ibis or baboon, body of a man

OSIRIS

God of the underworld and vegetation, often shown with a pharaoh's beard and mummy-wrapped legs. He is known for coming back to life after his brother, Set, killed him.

Appearance: Man with green, blue, or black skin

SEKHMET

Fire-breathing goddess of warfare, disease, and healing. Sekhmet was the daughter of the sun god, Ra, and sent to destroy his enemies.

Appearance: Head of a lioness, body of a woman

ISIS

Goddess of marriage, fertility, and magic. Isis gathered the scattered pieces of her husband Osiris and put him back together again. She is the mother of Horus.

Appearance: Woman

SET

God of deserts, storms, and violence. Set is most known for killing his brother Osiris and cutting him into pieces so he could win the throne of Egypt.

Appearance: Human, with the head of an unidentifiable animal

HOW TO BUILD A PYRAMID

There are around 80 pyramids still standing in Egypt, the most famous of them being the Great Pyramid of Giza. But much of its construction is still shrouded in mystery.

CONSTRUCTION

The Great Pyramid of Giza was built from more than two million blocks of limestone, excavated from a nearby quarry with stone hammers. Much harder granite and basalt blocks were used for the interior chambers and passages. They had to be floated down the Nile in boats, before being hauled up ramps on wooden sledges.

The rough blocks were then covered in a layer of imported white limestone that has since worn off. Today we only see the rough, stepped core of the pyramid, but it would have been polished to a blindingly white, smooth sheen.

Building such a wonder in ancient times was extremely hard work, and people thought for a long time that it was the work of thousands of slaves. However, historians now believe it was the result of many teams of paid skilled workers, who lived in dedicated worker villages. Despite living nearby, it still took over 20 years to build!

Pyramids were topped by a capstone, or pyramidion, that was covered in gold leaf and religious symbols.

479 feet tall when first built.

King's chamber

Queen's chamber

Each of the four points of the pyramid aligns to the points of the compass, which is super impressive considering compasses weren't around back then.

Underground chamber

THE AFTER LIFE

Pyramids were built as tombs for the ancient kings. Expensive items like gold, jewelry, clothes, and sometimes even unlucky slaves, were buried with their masters. These were all the things thought to be required to take into the afterlife with them.

Ancient Egyptians tried to live a good life, so that they could go on to the afterlife, which was a mirror-image of their life on Earth. When they died, the god Anubis guided their souls to the underworld where they could be judged by Osiris and other gods.

The dead person's heart was placed on the scales of justice and weighed against the feather of the goddess of truth, Ma'at. If the heart was equal to or lighter than the feather, they got to progress to the afterlife. But if the heart was heavier than the feather, it was devoured by a demon called Ammut.

Air vents

Entrance

The entrances were hidden, and traps and curses were placed within the pyramid to deter tomb robbers.

755 feet wide at the base when first built.

Each block weighed about 2.75 tons.

55

HIEROGLYPHICS

Ancient Egyptians wrote in symbols called hieroglyphics. It's one of the oldest forms of writing that historians know how to translate.

Hieroglyphics are unlike many alphabets in that each symbol can represent either a whole word, a part of a word, or a sound. But each symbol has multiple meanings, so it can be difficult to work out which one is being used. To make it even more complex, hieroglyphics can be read in lots of different ways—left to right, right to left, top to bottom or bottom to top. The way of working out which direction to read was by looking which way the hieroglyphs with eyes faced. Perhaps unsurprisingly, it took years to learn how to read and write, a role that was performed by scribes. They had to learn over 700 different hieroglyphs!

Use this simplified set of hieroglyphics to work out how to write your name, and send coded messages to your friends.

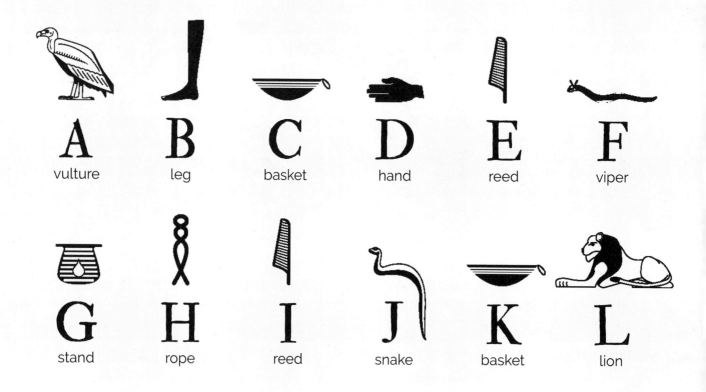

A	B	C	D	E	F
vulture	leg	basket	hand	reed	viper

G	H	I	J	K	L
stand	rope	reed	snake	basket	lion

M owl	**N** water	**O** lasso
P stool	**Q** hill	**R** mouth

S cloth	**T** loaf	**U** chick
W chick	**Y** reeds	**Z** door bolt

HOW TO COUNT LIKE AN ANCIENT EGYPTIAN

1			10
2			20
3			30
4			40
5			50
6			
7			100
8			
9			

MAKE YOUR OWN PAPYRUS PAPER

Try out the Ancient Egyptian method of making paper. You could even write messages on it using hieroglyphics.

The incredible papyrus is a grasslike plant that grows along the marshy Nile river. Ancient Egyptians used the stems of this plant to make a number of different things, such as baskets, mats, ropes, sandals, sails and, most importantly—paper.

People only wrote on one side of a sheet of papyrus, using a reed brush dipped in ink. When they ran out of space they attached another sheet to the bottom to create a long scroll that could be rolled up.

Ingredients

paper
1 cup plain flour
2 cups water
aluminum foil
rolling pin

I. Cut the paper into thin strips.

2. Mix flour and water in a small bowl to create a sort of "glue." Soak your strips of paper in the glue.

3. Lay half of the strips of paper vertically on a sheet of aluminum foil, squeezing the excess glue off the paper as you go.

4. Now lay the rest of the strips on top, horizontally.

5. Place another sheet of foil over the paper, and use a rolling pin or a bottle to squeeze out all the glue. This really sticks the paper together.

6. Peel back the foil and leave the paper to dry overnight before using.

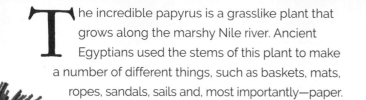

EGYPTIAN FOOD

Thanks to the fertile land along the Nile, Ancient Egyptians were able to grow an abundance of food, so even the very poor generally had enough to eat.

Ancient Egyptians ate two meals a day. One in the morning of bread and beer, and an evening meal of more bread and beer, along with lots of vegetables and fish. Wealthy people had more access to meat, such as pork, mutton, and even hippo and honey-roasted gazelle. A popular dish was hedgehog baked in clay—when the clay was cracked open, it took the sharp prickles with it. Fruit, such as figs, grapes, melon, and dates were generally eaten as dessert.

ANCIENT EGYPTIAN LUXURY DATE BALLS

Ingredients

7 oz. fresh pitted dates
3.5 oz. ground walnuts
3 tbsp honey
1 tsp cinnamon
Desiccated or
  shredded coconut

1. Add the dates, walnuts, and cinnamon to a blender and blend until smooth and sticky.

2. Use your hands to scoop out the sticky dough and form into bite-sized balls.

3. Place your date balls onto a baking tray and put them in the fridge for about 20 minutes.

4. Coat the date balls in a layer of honey, then roll the balls in a small bowl of desiccated coconut. Enjoy as an Ancient Egyptian inspired dessert or quick snack!

GLOSSARY

afterlife: the Ancient Egyptians believed that when they died, they would make a journey to a place of paradise called the Field of Reeds. They were buried with their earthly possessions so that they could take them into the afterlife with them.

burial chambers: when pharaohs and their families died, they were mummified and put into beautifully carved and decorated coffins, which were then placed in tombs or chambers, inside pyramids or buried in secret underground caverns or in high cliff rock faces.

canopic jars: clay pots used to hold the organs of the dead when their bodies were mummified. The jars were decorated with the animal heads of their gods.

embalming: the process of preserving a body by removing all the fluids and organs, before it is buried, so that it doesn't decompose (decay). The embalmed bodies are called mummies.

mummification: embalmed bodies were carefully covered in many layers of strips of linen wrapping, glued tightly together with resin. As the wrapped bodies were called mummies, this process of wrapping them in linen strips was known as mummification.

necropolis: a large, elaborately designed cemetery of an ancient city, filled with tombs and monuments to the honor the dead. The name comes from the Ancient Greek language and literally means "city of the dead."

hieroglyphics: an ancient writing system that uses pictures and symbols instead of letters and words.

Nubia: the name of a region of land along the River Nile, from Aswan to Khartoum, in Ancient Egyptian times. It was split into two parts, Upper Nubia (modern-day central Sudan) and Lower Nubia (modern-day southern Egypt and northern Sudan).

obelisk: a tall stone pillar, built in honor of a person or important event.

papyrus: a type of paper made from reeds.

pharaoh: the supreme leader, both politically and religiously, of the Ancient Egyptians. Pharaohs were seen as one of the gods and were worshipped as such.

pyramids: the stone tombs of the Ancient Egyptian pharaohs.

sarcophagus: the stone coffin that the mummy was put in.

scarab: a beetle found all over Ancient Egypt. The Ancient Egyptians believed the scarab beetle symbolized eternal life. They made stone scarabs as good luck charms or as pieces of jewelry.

scribe: a person who copies out written documents and manuscripts, especially before printing was invented.

shaduf: a hand-operated device for lifting water to irrigate crops.

vizier: the pharaoh's most important advisor, who helps rule the country.

FIND OUT MORE

Visit these museums, websites, and historic sites to discover more about the Ancient Egyptians.

MUSEUMS

SMITHSONIAN MUSEUM
Washington

THE MET MUSEUM
New York

FIELD MUSEUM
Chicago

ROSICRUCIAN EGYPTIAN MUSEUM
San Jose

PENN MUSEUM
Philadelphia

WEBSITES

BRITISH MUSEUM
www.britishmuseum.org/learn/schools/ages-7-11/ancient-egypt

NATIONAL GEOGRAPHIC KIDS
www.natgeokids.com/uk/discover/history/egypt/how-to-make-a-mummy

ROSICRUCIAN EGYPTIAN MUSEUM
egyptianmuseum.org/tomb-tour-exhibit

BBC BITESIZE
www.bbc.co.uk/bitesize/topics/zg87xnb

FABRICIUS – CREATE HIEROGLYPHIC MESSAGES
artsexperiments.withgoogle.com/fabricius/en/play/translator

VISITING EGYPT

GIZA NECROPOLIS
Site of the Great Pyramids and the Sphinx, an incredible part-human, part-lion, and part-eagle statue.

KARNAK
The largest religious temple ever built. Check out the 134 massive columns in the Great Hypostyle Hall.

VALLEY OF THE KINGS
Visit the burial chambers of the pharaohs, highly decorated with engravings and paintings. The tomb of Tutankhamun was found here.

ABU SIMBEL
Two massive temples in the city of Aswan, featuring four huge statues of Pharaoh Rameses II.

TEMPLE OF EDFU
One of the best preserved temples, located in the city of Edfu, dedicated to the god Horus.

TEMPLE OF PHILAE
This island temple, dedicated to the goddess Isis, was once completely underwater before being relocated to higher ground.

INDEX